50 Sushi Recipes for Beginners

By: Kelly Johnson

Table of Contents

- California Roll
- Cucumber Roll (Kappa Maki)
- Avocado Roll
- Salmon Nigiri
- Tuna Nigiri
- Shrimp Nigiri
- Spicy Tuna Roll
- Ebi (Shrimp) Roll
- Philadelphia Roll
- Dragon Roll
- Rainbow Roll
- Tempura Roll
- Vegetable Tempura Roll
- Spicy Crab Roll
- Unagi (Grilled Eel) Nigiri
- Tamago (Sweet Egg) Nigiri
- Scallop Nigiri
- Saba (Mackerel) Nigiri
- Ikura (Salmon Roe) Nigiri
- Seaweed Salad Roll
- Mango Avocado Roll
- Pork Belly Roll
- Crispy Rice Sushi
- Smoked Salmon Roll
- Beef Teriyaki Roll
- Zucchini Roll
- Pickled Radish Roll
- Tuna Tataki Roll
- Sushi Burrito
- Fruit Sushi
- Crispy Onion Roll
- Sesame Chicken Roll
- Baked Salmon Roll
- Tuna Sashimi
- Cabbage Roll

- Spicy Mayo Salmon Roll
- Shrimp Tempura Nigiri
- Vegetable Sushi
- Crab Stick Roll
- Pineapple Sushi
- Teriyaki Chicken Roll
- Sweet Potato Roll
- Sesame Spinach Roll
- Poke Bowl Sushi
- Kimchi Roll
- Quinoa Sushi
- Cilantro Lime Shrimp Roll
- Sushi Sandwich
- Sweet Chili Sauce Roll
- Coconut Shrimp Roll

California Roll

Ingredients

- **For the Sushi Rice:**
    - 2 cups sushi rice
    - 2 ½ cups water
    - ¼ cup rice vinegar
    - 2 tablespoons sugar
    - 1 teaspoon salt
- **For the Filling:**
    - 1 cup imitation crab meat (or cooked crab)
    - 1 medium avocado, sliced
    - 1 medium cucumber, julienned
    - Optional: 1 tablespoon mayonnaise (for a creamier texture)
- **For Rolling:**
    - 4 sheets of nori (seaweed)
    - Sesame seeds (optional)
    - Soy sauce (for serving)
    - Pickled ginger (for serving)
    - Wasabi (for serving)

Equipment

- Bamboo sushi mat
- Plastic wrap
- Sharp knife

Instructions

Prepare the Sushi Rice

1. **Rinse the Rice:** Rinse the sushi rice under cold water until the water runs clear to remove excess starch.
2. **Cook the Rice:** Combine the rinsed rice and water in a rice cooker. Cook according to the rice cooker's instructions. If using a stovetop, bring to a boil, then reduce to low heat, cover, and simmer for about 20 minutes.
3. **Season the Rice:** In a small saucepan, heat the rice vinegar, sugar, and salt over low heat until dissolved. Once the rice is cooked, transfer it to a large bowl and gently fold in the vinegar mixture. Allow it to cool to room temperature.

Assemble the California Rolls

1. **Prepare the Rolling Mat:** Place a sheet of plastic wrap over your bamboo sushi mat to prevent sticking.
2. **Place the Nori:** Lay a sheet of nori, shiny side down, on the plastic wrap.
3. **Spread the Rice:** Wet your hands to prevent sticking, then grab a handful of sushi rice and spread it evenly over the nori, leaving about 1 inch at the top edge.
4. **Add Fillings:** In the center of the rice, add a line of imitation crab, avocado slices, and cucumber sticks. If desired, drizzle a bit of mayonnaise over the filling.
5. **Roll the Sushi:** Starting from the bottom, lift the edge of the mat and begin rolling the sushi away from you, applying gentle pressure to form a tight roll. Continue rolling until you reach the exposed edge of the nori. Moisten the edge with a little water to seal it.
6. **Slice the Roll:** Using a sharp knife, slice the roll into 6-8 pieces. Wipe the knife with a damp cloth between cuts to ensure clean edges.

Serve

- Arrange the California rolls on a platter, sprinkle with sesame seeds (if using), and serve with soy sauce, pickled ginger, and wasabi on the side.

Enjoy your homemade California Rolls!

Cucumber Roll (Kappa Maki)

Ingredients

- **For the Sushi Rice:**
    - 2 cups sushi rice
    - 2 ½ cups water
    - ¼ cup rice vinegar
    - 2 tablespoons sugar
    - 1 teaspoon salt
- **For the Filling:**
    - 1 medium cucumber, julienned
- **For Rolling:**
    - 4 sheets of nori (seaweed)
    - Sesame seeds (optional)
    - Soy sauce (for serving)
    - Pickled ginger (for serving)
    - Wasabi (for serving)

Instructions

1. **Prepare the Sushi Rice:**
    - Rinse the sushi rice under cold water until the water runs clear.
    - Cook the rice in a rice cooker or stovetop as described previously.
    - Season the rice with rice vinegar, sugar, and salt, and allow it to cool to room temperature.
2. **Assemble the Cucumber Rolls:**
    - Place a sheet of plastic wrap on your bamboo sushi mat.
    - Lay a sheet of nori, shiny side down, on the plastic wrap.
    - Wet your hands and spread a handful of sushi rice evenly over the nori, leaving about 1 inch at the top.
    - Place a line of julienned cucumber in the center of the rice.
    - Roll the sushi away from you, applying gentle pressure, and seal the edge with a little water.
    - Slice the roll into 6-8 pieces and serve with soy sauce, pickled ginger, and wasabi.

Avocado Roll

Ingredients

- **For the Sushi Rice:**
    - 2 cups sushi rice
    - 2 ½ cups water
    - ¼ cup rice vinegar
    - 2 tablespoons sugar
    - 1 teaspoon salt
- **For the Filling:**
    - 1 medium avocado, sliced
- **For Rolling:**
    - 4 sheets of nori (seaweed)
    - Sesame seeds (optional)
    - Soy sauce (for serving)
    - Pickled ginger (for serving)
    - Wasabi (for serving)

Instructions

1. **Prepare the Sushi Rice:**
    - Rinse the sushi rice under cold water until the water runs clear.
    - Cook the rice in a rice cooker or stovetop as described previously.
    - Season the rice with rice vinegar, sugar, and salt, and allow it to cool to room temperature.
2. **Assemble the Avocado Rolls:**
    - Place a sheet of plastic wrap on your bamboo sushi mat.
    - Lay a sheet of nori, shiny side down, on the plastic wrap.
    - Wet your hands and spread a handful of sushi rice evenly over the nori, leaving about 1 inch at the top.
    - Place a line of avocado slices in the center of the rice.
    - Roll the sushi away from you, applying gentle pressure, and seal the edge with a little water.
    - Slice the roll into 6-8 pieces and serve with soy sauce, pickled ginger, and wasabi.

Salmon Nigiri

Ingredients

- **For the Sushi Rice:**
    - 2 cups sushi rice
    - 2 ½ cups water
    - ¼ cup rice vinegar
    - 2 tablespoons sugar
    - 1 teaspoon salt
- **For the Topping:**
    - 8 ounces fresh sushi-grade salmon, sliced thinly
- **For Serving:**
    - Soy sauce
    - Pickled ginger
    - Wasabi

Instructions

1. **Prepare the Sushi Rice:**
    - Rinse the sushi rice under cold water until the water runs clear.
    - Cook the rice in a rice cooker or stovetop as described previously.
    - Season the rice with rice vinegar, sugar, and salt, and allow it to cool to room temperature.
2. **Form the Nigiri:**
    - Wet your hands and take a small amount of sushi rice (about 2 tablespoons).
    - Gently form the rice into an oval shape by pressing it lightly between your palms.
    - Place a slice of salmon on top of the rice, pressing down gently to adhere.
3. **Serve:**
    - Arrange the salmon nigiri on a plate and serve with soy sauce, pickled ginger, and wasabi.

Enjoy your homemade sushi!

Tuna Nigiri

Ingredients

- **For the Sushi Rice:**
    - 2 cups sushi rice
    - 2 ½ cups water
    - ¼ cup rice vinegar
    - 2 tablespoons sugar
    - 1 teaspoon salt
- **For the Topping:**
    - 8 ounces fresh sushi-grade tuna, sliced thinly
- **For Serving:**
    - Soy sauce
    - Pickled ginger
    - Wasabi

Instructions

1. **Prepare the Sushi Rice:**
    - Rinse the sushi rice under cold water until the water runs clear.
    - Cook the rice in a rice cooker or stovetop as described previously.
    - Season the rice with rice vinegar, sugar, and salt, and allow it to cool to room temperature.
2. **Form the Nigiri:**
    - Wet your hands and take a small amount of sushi rice (about 2 tablespoons).
    - Gently form the rice into an oval shape by pressing it lightly between your palms.
    - Place a slice of tuna on top of the rice, pressing down gently to adhere.
3. **Serve:**
    - Arrange the tuna nigiri on a plate and serve with soy sauce, pickled ginger, and wasabi.

Shrimp Nigiri

Ingredients

- **For the Sushi Rice:**
    - 2 cups sushi rice
    - 2 ½ cups water
    - ¼ cup rice vinegar
    - 2 tablespoons sugar
    - 1 teaspoon salt
- **For the Topping:**
    - 8 ounces cooked shrimp, peeled and deveined
- **For Serving:**
    - Soy sauce
    - Pickled ginger
    - Wasabi

Instructions

1. **Prepare the Sushi Rice:**
    - Rinse the sushi rice under cold water until the water runs clear.
    - Cook the rice in a rice cooker or stovetop as described previously.
    - Season the rice with rice vinegar, sugar, and salt, and allow it to cool to room temperature.
2. **Form the Nigiri:**
    - Wet your hands and take a small amount of sushi rice (about 2 tablespoons).
    - Gently form the rice into an oval shape by pressing it lightly between your palms.
    - Place a shrimp on top of the rice, pressing down gently to adhere.
3. **Serve:**
    - Arrange the shrimp nigiri on a plate and serve with soy sauce, pickled ginger, and wasabi.

Spicy Tuna Roll

Ingredients

- **For the Sushi Rice:**
    - 2 cups sushi rice
    - 2 ½ cups water
    - ¼ cup rice vinegar
    - 2 tablespoons sugar
    - 1 teaspoon salt
- **For the Filling:**
    - 8 ounces sushi-grade tuna, diced
    - 2 tablespoons mayonnaise
    - 1 teaspoon sriracha (adjust to taste)
    - 1 green onion, chopped
- **For Rolling:**
    - 4 sheets of nori (seaweed)
    - Sesame seeds (optional)
    - Soy sauce (for serving)
    - Pickled ginger (for serving)
    - Wasabi (for serving)

Instructions

1. **Prepare the Sushi Rice:**
    - Rinse the sushi rice under cold water until the water runs clear.
    - Cook the rice in a rice cooker or stovetop as described previously.
    - Season the rice with rice vinegar, sugar, and salt, and allow it to cool to room temperature.
2. **Make the Spicy Tuna Filling:**
    - In a bowl, combine the diced tuna, mayonnaise, sriracha, and green onion. Mix well.
3. **Assemble the Spicy Tuna Rolls:**
    - Place a sheet of plastic wrap on your bamboo sushi mat.
    - Lay a sheet of nori, shiny side down, on the plastic wrap.
    - Wet your hands and spread a handful of sushi rice evenly over the nori, leaving about 1 inch at the top.
    - Place a line of spicy tuna filling in the center of the rice.
    - Roll the sushi away from you, applying gentle pressure, and seal the edge with a little water.

- Slice the roll into 6-8 pieces and serve with soy sauce, pickled ginger, and wasabi.

Ebi (Shrimp) Roll

Ingredients

- **For the Sushi Rice:**
    - 2 cups sushi rice
    - 2 ½ cups water
    - ¼ cup rice vinegar
    - 2 tablespoons sugar
    - 1 teaspoon salt
- **For the Filling:**
    - 8 ounces cooked shrimp, halved lengthwise
    - 1 cucumber, julienned
- **For Rolling:**
    - 4 sheets of nori (seaweed)
    - Sesame seeds (optional)
    - Soy sauce (for serving)
    - Pickled ginger (for serving)
    - Wasabi (for serving)

Instructions

1. **Prepare the Sushi Rice:**
    - Rinse the sushi rice under cold water until the water runs clear.
    - Cook the rice in a rice cooker or stovetop as described previously.
    - Season the rice with rice vinegar, sugar, and salt, and allow it to cool to room temperature.
2. **Assemble the Ebi Rolls:**
    - Place a sheet of plastic wrap on your bamboo sushi mat.
    - Lay a sheet of nori, shiny side down, on the plastic wrap.
    - Wet your hands and spread a handful of sushi rice evenly over the nori, leaving about 1 inch at the top.
    - Place a line of halved shrimp and cucumber in the center of the rice.
    - Roll the sushi away from you, applying gentle pressure, and seal the edge with a little water.
    - Slice the roll into 6-8 pieces and serve with soy sauce, pickled ginger, and wasabi.

Philadelphia Roll

Ingredients

- **For the Sushi Rice:**
    - 2 cups sushi rice
    - 2 ½ cups water
    - ¼ cup rice vinegar
    - 2 tablespoons sugar
    - 1 teaspoon salt
- **For the Filling:**
    - 4 ounces cream cheese, cut into strips
    - 1 medium cucumber, julienned
    - 8 ounces smoked salmon
- **For Rolling:**
    - 4 sheets of nori (seaweed)
    - Sesame seeds (optional)
    - Soy sauce (for serving)
    - Pickled ginger (for serving)
    - Wasabi (for serving)

Instructions

1. **Prepare the Sushi Rice:**
    - Rinse the sushi rice under cold water until the water runs clear.
    - Cook the rice in a rice cooker or stovetop as described previously.
    - Season the rice with rice vinegar, sugar, and salt, and allow it to cool to room temperature.
2. **Assemble the Philadelphia Rolls:**
    - Place a sheet of plastic wrap on your bamboo sushi mat.
    - Lay a sheet of nori, shiny side down, on the plastic wrap.
    - Wet your hands and spread a handful of sushi rice evenly over the nori, leaving about 1 inch at the top.
    - Place a line of cream cheese, cucumber, and smoked salmon in the center of the rice.
    - Roll the sushi away from you, applying gentle pressure, and seal the edge with a little water.
    - Slice the roll into 6-8 pieces and serve with soy sauce, pickled ginger, and wasabi.

Dragon Roll

Ingredients

- **For the Sushi Rice:**
    - 2 cups sushi rice
    - 2 ½ cups water
    - ¼ cup rice vinegar
    - 2 tablespoons sugar
    - 1 teaspoon salt
- **For the Filling:**
    - 8 ounces eel (unagi) or shrimp tempura
    - 1 medium cucumber, julienned
    - 1 avocado, sliced
- **For the Topping:**
    - 1 avocado, sliced (for decoration)
    - Eel sauce (for drizzling)
    - Sesame seeds (optional)
- **For Rolling:**
    - 4 sheets of nori (seaweed)
    - Soy sauce (for serving)
    - Pickled ginger (for serving)
    - Wasabi (for serving)

Instructions

1. **Prepare the Sushi Rice:**
    - Rinse the sushi rice under cold water until the water runs clear.
    - Cook the rice in a rice cooker or stovetop as described previously.
    - Season the rice with rice vinegar, sugar, and salt, and allow it to cool to room temperature.
2. **Assemble the Dragon Rolls:**
    - Place a sheet of plastic wrap on your bamboo sushi mat.
    - Lay a sheet of nori, shiny side down, on the plastic wrap.
    - Wet your hands and spread a handful of sushi rice evenly over the nori, leaving about 1 inch at the top.
    - Place a line of eel (or shrimp tempura) and cucumber in the center of the rice.
    - Roll the sushi away from you, applying gentle pressure, and seal the edge with a little water.

- Once rolled, place sliced avocado on top of the roll and press gently to adhere.
- Drizzle with eel sauce and sprinkle sesame seeds if desired. Slice the roll into 6-8 pieces and serve with soy sauce, pickled ginger, and wasabi.

Rainbow Roll

Ingredients

- **For the Sushi Rice:**
    - 2 cups sushi rice
    - 2 ½ cups water
    - ¼ cup rice vinegar
    - 2 tablespoons sugar
    - 1 teaspoon salt
- **For the Filling:**
    - 4 ounces crab meat (or imitation crab)
    - 1 avocado, sliced
    - 1 cucumber, julienned
- **For the Topping:**
    - 4 ounces assorted sashimi (tuna, salmon, yellowtail, etc.), sliced
- **For Rolling:**
    - 4 sheets of nori (seaweed)
    - Soy sauce (for serving)
    - Pickled ginger (for serving)
    - Wasabi (for serving)

Instructions

1. **Prepare the Sushi Rice:**
    - Rinse the sushi rice under cold water until the water runs clear.
    - Cook the rice in a rice cooker or stovetop as described previously.
    - Season the rice with rice vinegar, sugar, and salt, and allow it to cool to room temperature.
2. **Assemble the Rainbow Rolls:**
    - Place a sheet of plastic wrap on your bamboo sushi mat.
    - Lay a sheet of nori, shiny side down, on the plastic wrap.
    - Wet your hands and spread a handful of sushi rice evenly over the nori, leaving about 1 inch at the top.
    - Place a line of crab meat, avocado, and cucumber in the center of the rice.
    - Roll the sushi away from you, applying gentle pressure, and seal the edge with a little water.
    - Once rolled, place assorted sashimi slices on top of the roll and press gently to adhere.

- Slice the roll into 6-8 pieces and serve with soy sauce, pickled ginger, and wasabi.

Tempura Roll

Ingredients

- **For the Sushi Rice:**
    - 2 cups sushi rice
    - 2 ½ cups water
    - ¼ cup rice vinegar
    - 2 tablespoons sugar
    - 1 teaspoon salt
- **For the Tempura Filling:**
    - 8 ounces assorted vegetables (sweet potato, zucchini, bell pepper)
    - 1 cup tempura batter mix
    - Water (as directed on batter mix)
- **For Rolling:**
    - 4 sheets of nori (seaweed)
    - Soy sauce (for serving)
    - Pickled ginger (for serving)
    - Wasabi (for serving)

Instructions

1. **Prepare the Sushi Rice:**
    - Rinse the sushi rice under cold water until the water runs clear.
    - Cook the rice in a rice cooker or stovetop as described previously.
    - Season the rice with rice vinegar, sugar, and salt, and allow it to cool to room temperature.
2. **Prepare the Tempura:**
    - Heat oil in a deep fryer or heavy pot to 350°F (175°C).
    - Dip the vegetables into the tempura batter and fry until golden brown. Drain on paper towels.
3. **Assemble the Tempura Rolls:**
    - Place a sheet of plastic wrap on your bamboo sushi mat.
    - Lay a sheet of nori, shiny side down, on the plastic wrap.
    - Wet your hands and spread a handful of sushi rice evenly over the nori, leaving about 1 inch at the top.
    - Place tempura vegetables in the center of the rice.
    - Roll the sushi away from you, applying gentle pressure, and seal the edge with a little water.

    - Slice the roll into 6-8 pieces and serve with soy sauce, pickled ginger, and wasabi.

Vegetable Tempura Roll

Ingredients

- **For the Sushi Rice:**
  - 2 cups sushi rice
  - 2 ½ cups water
  - ¼ cup rice vinegar
  - 2 tablespoons sugar
  - 1 teaspoon salt
- **For the Tempura Filling:**
  - 1 medium zucchini, julienned
  - 1 medium sweet potato, julienned
  - 1 bell pepper, julienned
  - 1 cup tempura batter mix
  - Water (as directed on batter mix)
- **For Rolling:**
  - 4 sheets of nori (seaweed)
  - Soy sauce (for serving)
  - Pickled ginger (for serving)
  - Wasabi (for serving)

Instructions

1. **Prepare the Sushi Rice:**
   - Rinse the sushi rice under cold water until the water runs clear.
   - Cook the rice in a rice cooker or stovetop as described previously.
   - Season the rice with rice vinegar, sugar, and salt, and allow it to cool to room temperature.
2. **Prepare the Vegetable Tempura:**
   - Heat oil in a deep fryer or heavy pot to 350°F (175°C).
   - Dip the vegetables into the tempura batter and fry until golden brown. Drain on paper towels.
3. **Assemble the Vegetable Tempura Rolls:**
   - Place a sheet of plastic wrap on your bamboo sushi mat.
   - Lay a sheet of nori, shiny side down, on the plastic wrap.
   - Wet your hands and spread a handful of sushi rice evenly over the nori, leaving about 1 inch at the top.
   - Place tempura vegetables in the center of the rice.

    - Roll the sushi away from you, applying gentle pressure, and seal the edge with a little water.
    - Slice the roll into 6-8 pieces and serve with soy sauce, pickled ginger, and wasabi.

Enjoy your sushi-making adventure!

Spicy Crab Roll

Ingredients

- **For the Sushi Rice:**
    - 2 cups sushi rice
    - 2 ½ cups water
    - ¼ cup rice vinegar
    - 2 tablespoons sugar
    - 1 teaspoon salt
- **For the Filling:**
    - 8 ounces crab meat (or imitation crab)
    - 2 tablespoons mayonnaise
    - 1 tablespoon Sriracha (adjust for spice level)
    - 1 avocado, sliced
    - 1 cucumber, julienned
- **For Rolling:**
    - 4 sheets of nori (seaweed)
    - Soy sauce (for serving)
    - Pickled ginger (for serving)
    - Wasabi (for serving)

Instructions

1. **Prepare the Sushi Rice:**
    - Rinse the sushi rice under cold water until the water runs clear.
    - Cook the rice in a rice cooker or stovetop as described previously.
    - Season the rice with rice vinegar, sugar, and salt, and allow it to cool to room temperature.
2. **Mix the Crab Filling:**
    - In a bowl, combine the crab meat, mayonnaise, and Sriracha. Mix well.
3. **Assemble the Roll:**
    - Place a sheet of plastic wrap on your bamboo sushi mat.
    - Lay a sheet of nori, shiny side down, on the plastic wrap.
    - Wet your hands and spread a handful of sushi rice evenly over the nori, leaving about 1 inch at the top.
    - In the center, add a line of the spicy crab mixture, avocado slices, and cucumber.
    - Roll the sushi away from you, applying gentle pressure, and seal the edge with a little water.

- Slice the roll into 6-8 pieces and serve with soy sauce, pickled ginger, and wasabi.

Unagi (Grilled Eel) Nigiri

Ingredients

- 8 ounces unagi (grilled eel), sliced
- **For the Sushi Rice:**
    - 2 cups sushi rice
    - 2 ½ cups water
    - ¼ cup rice vinegar
    - 2 tablespoons sugar
    - 1 teaspoon salt
- Soy sauce (for serving)
- Optional: thinly sliced green onions for garnish

Instructions

1. **Prepare the Sushi Rice:**
    - Rinse the sushi rice under cold water until the water runs clear.
    - Cook the rice as previously described, then season with rice vinegar, sugar, and salt, and allow it to cool.
2. **Shape the Nigiri:**
    - Wet your hands and take a small amount of sushi rice (about 2 tablespoons) and shape it into an oval mound.
    - Top the rice with a slice of unagi.
    - If desired, garnish with thinly sliced green onions.
3. **Serve:**
    - Serve with soy sauce and enjoy.

Tamago (Sweet Egg) Nigiri

Ingredients

- **For the Tamago (Egg Omelet):**
    - 4 large eggs
    - 2 tablespoons sugar
    - 1 tablespoon soy sauce
    - 1 tablespoon mirin (optional)
    - Oil (for frying)
- **For the Sushi Rice:**
    - 2 cups sushi rice
    - 2 ½ cups water
    - ¼ cup rice vinegar
    - 2 tablespoons sugar
    - 1 teaspoon salt

Instructions

1. **Prepare the Sushi Rice:**
    - Rinse the sushi rice under cold water until the water runs clear.
    - Cook the rice as previously described, then season and cool it.
2. **Make the Tamago:**
    - In a bowl, whisk together eggs, sugar, soy sauce, and mirin.
    - Heat a small amount of oil in a nonstick skillet over medium heat.
    - Pour in a thin layer of the egg mixture and cook until set. Roll the omelet and push it to one side of the pan.
    - Repeat with more egg mixture, rolling each layer over the previous one until all the mixture is used.
    - Once cooked, let it cool and slice into rectangular pieces.
3. **Shape the Nigiri:**
    - Wet your hands and shape sushi rice into small oval mounds.
    - Place a slice of tamago on top of each mound.
4. **Serve:**
    - Enjoy with soy sauce.

Scallop Nigiri

Ingredients

- 8 ounces fresh scallops, sliced
- **For the Sushi Rice:**
    - 2 cups sushi rice
    - 2 ½ cups water
    - ¼ cup rice vinegar
    - 2 tablespoons sugar
    - 1 teaspoon salt
- Soy sauce (for serving)

Instructions

1. **Prepare the Sushi Rice:**
    - Rinse and cook the sushi rice as previously described, then season and cool it.
2. **Shape the Nigiri:**
    - Wet your hands and take small portions of rice, shaping them into oval mounds.
    - Top each mound with a slice of scallop.
3. **Serve:**
    - Serve with soy sauce.

Saba (Mackerel) Nigiri

Ingredients

- 8 ounces saba (mackerel), filleted and cured
- **For the Sushi Rice:**
    - 2 cups sushi rice
    - 2 ½ cups water
    - ¼ cup rice vinegar
    - 2 tablespoons sugar
    - 1 teaspoon salt
- Soy sauce (for serving)

Instructions

1. **Prepare the Sushi Rice:**
    - Rinse and cook the sushi rice as previously described, then season and cool it.
2. **Shape the Nigiri:**
    - Wet your hands and shape small portions of rice into oval mounds.
    - Place a slice of saba on top of each mound.
3. **Serve:**
    - Enjoy with soy sauce.

Ikura (Salmon Roe) Nigiri

Ingredients

- 8 ounces ikura (salmon roe)
- **For the Sushi Rice:**
    - 2 cups sushi rice
    - 2 ½ cups water
    - ¼ cup rice vinegar
    - 2 tablespoons sugar
    - 1 teaspoon salt
- Soy sauce (for serving)

Instructions

1. **Prepare the Sushi Rice:**
    - Rinse and cook the sushi rice as previously described, then season and cool it.
2. **Shape the Nigiri:**
    - Wet your hands and shape small portions of rice into oval mounds.
    - Top each mound with a spoonful of ikura.
3. **Serve:**
    - Serve with soy sauce.

Seaweed Salad Roll

Ingredients

- **For the Sushi Rice:**
    - 2 cups sushi rice
    - 2 ½ cups water
    - ¼ cup rice vinegar
    - 2 tablespoons sugar
    - 1 teaspoon salt
- **For the Filling:**
    - 1 cup prepared seaweed salad (store-bought or homemade)
    - 1 cucumber, julienned
    - 1 avocado, sliced
- **For Rolling:**
    - 4 sheets of nori (seaweed)
    - Soy sauce (for serving)
    - Pickled ginger (for serving)
    - Wasabi (for serving)

Instructions

1. **Prepare the Sushi Rice:**
    - Rinse and cook the sushi rice as previously described, then season and cool it.
2. **Assemble the Roll:**
    - Place a sheet of plastic wrap on your bamboo sushi mat.
    - Lay a sheet of nori, shiny side down, on the plastic wrap.
    - Wet your hands and spread a handful of sushi rice evenly over the nori, leaving about 1 inch at the top.
    - In the center, add a line of seaweed salad, cucumber, and avocado.
    - Roll the sushi away from you, applying gentle pressure, and seal the edge with a little water.
    - Slice the roll into 6-8 pieces and serve with soy sauce, pickled ginger, and wasabi.

Mango Avocado Roll

Ingredients

- **For the Sushi Rice:**
    - 2 cups sushi rice
    - 2 ½ cups water
    - ¼ cup rice vinegar
    - 2 tablespoons sugar
    - 1 teaspoon salt
- **For the Filling:**
    - 1 ripe mango, sliced
    - 1 avocado, sliced
    - Optional: cream cheese (for a richer flavor)
- **For Rolling:**
    - 4 sheets of nori (seaweed)
    - Soy sauce (for serving)
    - Pickled ginger (for serving)
    - Wasabi (for serving)

Instructions

1. **Prepare the Sushi Rice:**
    - Rinse and cook the sushi rice as previously described, then season and cool it.
2. **Assemble the Roll:**
    - Place a sheet of plastic wrap on your bamboo sushi mat.
    - Lay a sheet of nori, shiny side down, on the plastic wrap.
    - Wet your hands and spread a handful of sushi rice evenly over the nori, leaving about 1 inch at the top.
    - In the center, add slices of mango and avocado. If desired, add a thin layer of cream cheese.
    - Roll the sushi away from you, applying gentle pressure, and seal the edge with a little water.
    - Slice the roll into 6-8 pieces and serve with soy sauce, pickled ginger, and wasabi.

Pork Belly Roll

Ingredients

- **For the Sushi Rice:**
    - 2 cups sushi rice
    - 2 ½ cups water
    - ¼ cup rice vinegar
    - 2 tablespoons sugar
    - 1 teaspoon salt
- **For the Filling:**
    - 8 ounces cooked pork belly, sliced thin
    - 1 cucumber, julienned
    - 1 avocado, sliced
    - 1 tablespoon hoisin sauce (optional)
- **For Rolling:**
    - 4 sheets of nori (seaweed)
    - Soy sauce (for serving)
    - Pickled ginger (for serving)
    - Wasabi (for serving)

Instructions

1. **Prepare the Sushi Rice:**
    - Rinse and cook the sushi rice as previously described, then season and cool it.
2. **Assemble the Roll:**
    - Place a sheet of plastic wrap on your bamboo sushi mat.
    - Lay a sheet of nori, shiny side down, on the plastic wrap.
    - Wet your hands and spread a handful of sushi rice evenly over the nori, leaving about 1 inch at the top.
    - In the center, add slices of pork belly, cucumber, and avocado. Drizzle with hoisin sauce if desired.
    - Roll the sushi away from you, applying gentle pressure, and seal the edge with a little water.
    - Slice the roll into 6-8 pieces and serve with soy sauce, pickled ginger, and wasabi.

Crispy Rice Sushi

Ingredients

- **For the Sushi Rice:**
    - 2 cups sushi rice
    - 2 ½ cups water
    - ¼ cup rice vinegar
    - 2 tablespoons sugar
    - 1 teaspoon salt
- **For Topping:**
    - 8 ounces cooked shrimp or spicy tuna (prepared)
    - ¼ cup mayonnaise (optional, for a creamy texture)
    - 1 tablespoon Sriracha (optional, for spice)
    - Green onions, chopped (for garnish)
    - Furikake seasoning (for garnish)
- **For Frying:**
    - Vegetable oil (for frying)

Instructions

1. **Prepare the Sushi Rice:**
    - Rinse the sushi rice under cold water until the water runs clear.
    - Cook the rice as described previously, then season with rice vinegar, sugar, and salt, and allow it to cool.
2. **Shape the Rice:**
    - Once cooled, wet your hands and form the sushi rice into rectangular or square blocks.
3. **Fry the Rice:**
    - Heat vegetable oil in a pan over medium heat.
    - Carefully place the rice blocks in the hot oil and fry until golden brown on both sides. Remove and drain on paper towels.
4. **Top and Serve:**
    - Mix the cooked shrimp or spicy tuna with mayonnaise and Sriracha.
    - Spoon the mixture onto each crispy rice block.
    - Garnish with green onions and furikake. Serve immediately.

Smoked Salmon Roll

Ingredients

- **For the Sushi Rice:**
    - 2 cups sushi rice
    - 2 ½ cups water
    - ¼ cup rice vinegar
    - 2 tablespoons sugar
    - 1 teaspoon salt
- **For the Filling:**
    - 8 ounces smoked salmon
    - 1 cucumber, julienned
    - 1 avocado, sliced
    - Cream cheese (optional)
- **For Rolling:**
    - 4 sheets of nori (seaweed)
    - Soy sauce (for serving)
    - Pickled ginger (for serving)
    - Wasabi (for serving)

Instructions

1. **Prepare the Sushi Rice:**
    - Rinse the sushi rice under cold water until the water runs clear.
    - Cook and season the rice as previously described, then allow it to cool.
2. **Assemble the Roll:**
    - Place a sheet of plastic wrap on your bamboo sushi mat.
    - Lay a sheet of nori, shiny side down, on the plastic wrap.
    - Wet your hands and spread a handful of sushi rice evenly over the nori, leaving about 1 inch at the top.
    - In the center, layer smoked salmon, cucumber, avocado, and a thin layer of cream cheese if desired.
    - Roll the sushi away from you, applying gentle pressure, and seal the edge with a little water.
    - Slice the roll into 6-8 pieces and serve with soy sauce, pickled ginger, and wasabi.

Beef Teriyaki Roll

Ingredients

- **For the Sushi Rice:**
    - 2 cups sushi rice
    - 2 ½ cups water
    - ¼ cup rice vinegar
    - 2 tablespoons sugar
    - 1 teaspoon salt
- **For the Filling:**
    - 8 ounces beef (flank steak or sirloin), cooked and sliced thin
    - ¼ cup teriyaki sauce
    - 1 cucumber, julienned
    - 1 avocado, sliced
- **For Rolling:**
    - 4 sheets of nori (seaweed)
    - Soy sauce (for serving)
    - Pickled ginger (for serving)
    - Wasabi (for serving)

Instructions

1. **Prepare the Sushi Rice:**
    - Rinse the sushi rice under cold water until the water runs clear.
    - Cook and season the rice as previously described, then allow it to cool.
2. **Marinate the Beef:**
    - In a bowl, mix the cooked beef with teriyaki sauce.
3. **Assemble the Roll:**
    - Place a sheet of plastic wrap on your bamboo sushi mat.
    - Lay a sheet of nori, shiny side down, on the plastic wrap.
    - Wet your hands and spread a handful of sushi rice evenly over the nori, leaving about 1 inch at the top.
    - In the center, layer the marinated beef, cucumber, and avocado.
    - Roll the sushi away from you, applying gentle pressure, and seal the edge with a little water.
    - Slice the roll into 6-8 pieces and serve with soy sauce, pickled ginger, and wasabi.

Zucchini Roll

Ingredients

- **For the Sushi Rice:**
    - 2 cups sushi rice
    - 2 ½ cups water
    - ¼ cup rice vinegar
    - 2 tablespoons sugar
    - 1 teaspoon salt
- **For the Filling:**
    - 1 medium zucchini, julienned
    - 1 carrot, julienned
    - 1 bell pepper, sliced thin
    - 1 avocado, sliced
- **For Rolling:**
    - 4 sheets of nori (seaweed)
    - Soy sauce (for serving)
    - Pickled ginger (for serving)
    - Wasabi (for serving)

Instructions

1. **Prepare the Sushi Rice:**
    - Rinse the sushi rice under cold water until the water runs clear.
    - Cook and season the rice as previously described, then allow it to cool.
2. **Assemble the Roll:**
    - Place a sheet of plastic wrap on your bamboo sushi mat.
    - Lay a sheet of nori, shiny side down, on the plastic wrap.
    - Wet your hands and spread a handful of sushi rice evenly over the nori, leaving about 1 inch at the top.
    - In the center, layer the zucchini, carrot, bell pepper, and avocado.
    - Roll the sushi away from you, applying gentle pressure, and seal the edge with a little water.
    - Slice the roll into 6-8 pieces and serve with soy sauce, pickled ginger, and wasabi.

Pickled Radish Roll

Ingredients

- **For the Sushi Rice:**
    - 2 cups sushi rice
    - 2 ½ cups water
    - ¼ cup rice vinegar
    - 2 tablespoons sugar
    - 1 teaspoon salt
- **For the Filling:**
    - 1 cup pickled radish (danmuji), sliced
    - 1 cucumber, julienned
    - 1 avocado, sliced
- **For Rolling:**
    - 4 sheets of nori (seaweed)
    - Soy sauce (for serving)
    - Pickled ginger (for serving)
    - Wasabi (for serving)

Instructions

1. **Prepare the Sushi Rice:**
    - Rinse the sushi rice under cold water until the water runs clear.
    - Cook and season the rice as previously described, then allow it to cool.
2. **Assemble the Roll:**
    - Place a sheet of plastic wrap on your bamboo sushi mat.
    - Lay a sheet of nori, shiny side down, on the plastic wrap.
    - Wet your hands and spread a handful of sushi rice evenly over the nori, leaving about 1 inch at the top.
    - In the center, layer the pickled radish, cucumber, and avocado.
    - Roll the sushi away from you, applying gentle pressure, and seal the edge with a little water.
    - Slice the roll into 6-8 pieces and serve with soy sauce, pickled ginger, and wasabi.

Tuna Tataki Roll

Ingredients

- **For the Sushi Rice:**
    - 2 cups sushi rice
    - 2 ½ cups water
    - ¼ cup rice vinegar
    - 2 tablespoons sugar
    - 1 teaspoon salt
- **For the Filling:**
    - 8 ounces tuna steak, seared and sliced
    - 1 cucumber, julienned
    - 1 avocado, sliced
    - Soy sauce (for dipping)
    - Sesame seeds (for garnish)
- **For Rolling:**
    - 4 sheets of nori (seaweed)
    - Soy sauce (for serving)
    - Pickled ginger (for serving)
    - Wasabi (for serving)

Instructions

1. **Prepare the Sushi Rice:**
    - Rinse the sushi rice under cold water until the water runs clear.
    - Cook and season the rice as previously described, then allow it to cool.
2. **Assemble the Roll:**
    - Place a sheet of plastic wrap on your bamboo sushi mat.
    - Lay a sheet of nori, shiny side down, on the plastic wrap.
    - Wet your hands and spread a handful of sushi rice evenly over the nori, leaving about 1 inch at the top.
    - In the center, layer the sliced tuna, cucumber, and avocado.
    - Roll the sushi away from you, applying gentle pressure, and seal the edge with a little water.
    - Slice the roll into 6-8 pieces and garnish with sesame seeds. Serve with soy sauce, pickled ginger, and wasabi.

Sushi Burrito

Ingredients

- **For the Sushi Rice:**
    - 2 cups sushi rice
    - 2 ½ cups water
    - ¼ cup rice vinegar
    - 2 tablespoons sugar
    - 1 teaspoon salt
- **For the Filling:**
    - 8 ounces cooked shrimp, crab, or tofu
    - 1 cup mixed greens
    - 1 carrot, julienned
    - 1 cucumber, julienned
    - 1 avocado, sliced
    - Soy sauce (for dipping)
- **For Rolling:**
    - 2 large sheets of nori (seaweed)

Instructions

1. **Prepare the Sushi Rice:**
    - Rinse the sushi rice under cold water until the water runs clear.
    - Cook and season the rice as previously described, then allow it to cool.
2. **Assemble the Burrito:**
    - Place a sheet of plastic wrap on a clean surface.
    - Lay a sheet of nori, shiny side down, on the plastic wrap.
    - Wet your hands and spread a generous amount of sushi rice evenly over the nori, leaving about 1 inch at the top.
    - Layer the mixed greens, shrimp or crab, carrot, cucumber, and avocado in the center.
    - Roll the sushi tightly from the bottom to the top, using the plastic wrap to help. Seal the edge with a little water.
    - Slice the burrito in half and serve with soy sauce for dipping.

Fruit Sushi

Ingredients

- **For the Sushi Rice:**
    - 2 cups sushi rice
    - 2 ½ cups water
    - ¼ cup rice vinegar
    - 2 tablespoons sugar
    - 1 teaspoon salt
- **For the Filling:**
    - 1 mango, sliced
    - 1 kiwi, sliced
    - 1 banana, sliced
    - ¼ cup coconut flakes (optional)
- **For Rolling:**
    - 4 sheets of nori (seaweed) or fruit leather (for a sweeter option)

Instructions

1. **Prepare the Sushi Rice:**
    - Rinse the sushi rice under cold water until the water runs clear.
    - Cook and season the rice as previously described, then allow it to cool.
2. **Assemble the Roll:**
    - If using nori, place a sheet of plastic wrap on your bamboo sushi mat.
    - Lay a sheet of nori (or fruit leather) on the mat.
    - Wet your hands and spread a handful of sushi rice evenly over the nori, leaving about 1 inch at the top.
    - In the center, layer the slices of mango, kiwi, and banana. Sprinkle with coconut flakes if desired.
    - Roll the sushi away from you, applying gentle pressure, and seal the edge with a little water.
    - Slice the roll into 6-8 pieces and serve immediately.

Crispy Onion Roll

Ingredients

- **For the Sushi Rice:**
    - 2 cups sushi rice
    - 2 ½ cups water
    - ¼ cup rice vinegar
    - 2 tablespoons sugar
    - 1 teaspoon salt
- **For the Filling:**
    - 8 ounces cooked shrimp or crab
    - ½ cup crispy fried onions
    - 1 cucumber, julienned
    - 1 avocado, sliced
- **For Rolling:**
    - 4 sheets of nori (seaweed)
    - Soy sauce (for serving)
    - Pickled ginger (for serving)
    - Wasabi (for serving)

Instructions

1. **Prepare the Sushi Rice:**
    - Rinse the sushi rice under cold water until the water runs clear.
    - Cook and season the rice as previously described, then allow it to cool.
2. **Assemble the Roll:**
    - Place a sheet of plastic wrap on your bamboo sushi mat.
    - Lay a sheet of nori, shiny side down, on the plastic wrap.
    - Wet your hands and spread a handful of sushi rice evenly over the nori, leaving about 1 inch at the top.
    - In the center, layer the shrimp or crab, crispy fried onions, cucumber, and avocado.
    - Roll the sushi away from you, applying gentle pressure, and seal the edge with a little water.
    - Slice the roll into 6-8 pieces and serve with soy sauce, pickled ginger, and wasabi.

Sesame Chicken Roll

Ingredients

- **For the Sushi Rice:**
    - 2 cups sushi rice
    - 2 ½ cups water
    - ¼ cup rice vinegar
    - 2 tablespoons sugar
    - 1 teaspoon salt
- **For the Filling:**
    - 8 ounces cooked sesame chicken, diced
    - 1 cucumber, julienned
    - 1 avocado, sliced
- **For Rolling:**
    - 4 sheets of nori (seaweed)
    - Soy sauce (for serving)
    - Pickled ginger (for serving)
    - Wasabi (for serving)

Instructions

1. **Prepare the Sushi Rice:**
    - Rinse the sushi rice under cold water until the water runs clear.
    - Cook and season the rice as previously described, then allow it to cool.
2. **Assemble the Roll:**
    - Place a sheet of plastic wrap on your bamboo sushi mat.
    - Lay a sheet of nori, shiny side down, on the plastic wrap.
    - Wet your hands and spread a handful of sushi rice evenly over the nori, leaving about 1 inch at the top.
    - In the center, layer the sesame chicken, cucumber, and avocado.
    - Roll the sushi away from you, applying gentle pressure, and seal the edge with a little water.
    - Slice the roll into 6-8 pieces and serve with soy sauce, pickled ginger, and wasabi.

Baked Salmon Roll

Ingredients

- **For the Sushi Rice:**
    - 2 cups sushi rice
    - 2 ½ cups water
    - ¼ cup rice vinegar
    - 2 tablespoons sugar
    - 1 teaspoon salt
- **For the Filling:**
    - 8 ounces salmon fillet, cooked and flaked
    - 1 avocado, sliced
    - ½ cucumber, julienned
    - ½ cup cream cheese
- **For Topping:**
    - 1 tablespoon mayonnaise
    - 1 teaspoon sriracha (adjust to taste)
    - Sesame seeds for garnish
    - 4 sheets of nori (seaweed)

Instructions

1. **Prepare the Sushi Rice:**
    - Rinse the sushi rice under cold water until the water runs clear.
    - Cook the rice according to package instructions, then mix in vinegar, sugar, and salt. Allow to cool.
2. **Assemble the Roll:**
    - Preheat the oven to 350°F (175°C).
    - Place a sheet of plastic wrap on a bamboo sushi mat. Lay a sheet of nori on top, shiny side down.
    - Wet your hands and spread a layer of sushi rice over the nori, leaving a 1-inch border at the top.
    - In the center, add flaked salmon, avocado, cucumber, and cream cheese.
    - Roll tightly away from you, using the mat to help. Seal with a little water.
3. **Bake the Roll:**
    - Place the roll seam side down on a baking sheet.
    - Mix mayonnaise and sriracha, spreading it over the top of the roll.
    - Bake for 10-15 minutes until heated through.
    - Slice, garnish with sesame seeds, and serve.

Tuna Sashimi

Ingredients

- **For the Sashimi:**
    - 8 ounces sushi-grade tuna, sliced thin
    - Soy sauce (for dipping)
    - Wasabi (for serving)
    - Pickled ginger (for serving)

Instructions

1. **Prepare the Tuna:**
    - Ensure the tuna is sushi-grade and very fresh.
    - Using a sharp knife, slice the tuna into thin, even pieces.
2. **Serve:**
    - Arrange the slices on a plate. Serve with soy sauce, wasabi, and pickled ginger on the side.

Cabbage Roll

Ingredients

- **For the Rolls:**
    - 8 large cabbage leaves
    - 1 cup cooked rice
    - 1 pound ground beef or turkey
    - 1 small onion, diced
    - 1 carrot, grated
    - 1 teaspoon garlic powder
    - Salt and pepper to taste
- **For the Sauce:**
    - 1 can (15 ounces) tomato sauce
    - 1 tablespoon sugar
    - 1 tablespoon lemon juice
    - 1 teaspoon paprika

Instructions

1. **Prepare the Cabbage:**
    - Blanch cabbage leaves in boiling water for 2-3 minutes until softened. Remove and cool.
2. **Make the Filling:**
    - In a bowl, mix cooked rice, ground meat, onion, carrot, garlic powder, salt, and pepper.
3. **Assemble the Rolls:**
    - Place about 2 tablespoons of filling on each cabbage leaf and roll tightly, tucking in the sides.
4. **Cook:**
    - Preheat oven to 350°F (175°C).
    - Mix sauce ingredients and pour a layer into a baking dish. Place cabbage rolls seam side down in the dish, cover with remaining sauce, and bake for 45 minutes.

Spicy Mayo Salmon Roll

Ingredients

- **For the Sushi Rice:**
    - 2 cups sushi rice
    - 2 ½ cups water
    - ¼ cup rice vinegar
    - 2 tablespoons sugar
    - 1 teaspoon salt
- **For the Filling:**
    - 8 ounces cooked salmon, flaked
    - ½ avocado, sliced
    - ½ cucumber, julienned
    - 2 tablespoons spicy mayo (mix mayonnaise with sriracha)
- **For Rolling:**
    - 4 sheets of nori (seaweed)

Instructions

1. **Prepare the Sushi Rice:**
    - Rinse the sushi rice, cook it, and season as mentioned above. Allow to cool.
2. **Assemble the Roll:**
    - Lay a sheet of nori on a bamboo mat. Spread rice over it, leaving a 1-inch border.
    - In the center, layer salmon, avocado, cucumber, and drizzle with spicy mayo.
    - Roll tightly, seal, and slice.

Shrimp Tempura Nigiri

Ingredients

- **For the Sushi Rice:**
    - 2 cups sushi rice
    - 2 ½ cups water
    - ¼ cup rice vinegar
    - 2 tablespoons sugar
    - 1 teaspoon salt
- **For the Tempura:**
    - 10 large shrimp, peeled and deveined
    - 1 cup tempura batter mix
    - Oil for frying
- **For Serving:**
    - Soy sauce (for dipping)

Instructions

1. **Prepare the Sushi Rice:**
    - Rinse the sushi rice, cook it, and season as mentioned above. Allow to cool.
2. **Make Tempura:**
    - Heat oil in a deep pan. Prepare tempura batter according to package instructions.
    - Dip shrimp in batter and fry until golden. Drain on paper towels.
3. **Assemble Nigiri:**
    - Wet your hands and form small mounds of sushi rice. Top each mound with a piece of tempura shrimp.
    - Serve with soy sauce for dipping.

Vegetable Sushi

Ingredients

- **For the Sushi Rice:**
    - 2 cups sushi rice
    - 2 ½ cups water
    - ¼ cup rice vinegar
    - 2 tablespoons sugar
    - 1 teaspoon salt
- **For the Filling:**
    - 1 avocado, sliced
    - 1 carrot, julienned
    - 1 cucumber, julienned
    - ½ bell pepper, sliced
    - 1 cup mixed greens
- **For Rolling:**
    - 4 sheets of nori (seaweed)

Instructions

1. **Prepare the Sushi Rice:**
    - Rinse the sushi rice, cook it, and season as mentioned above. Allow to cool.
2. **Assemble the Roll:**
    - Lay a sheet of nori on a bamboo mat. Spread rice over it, leaving a 1-inch border.
    - Layer the avocado, carrot, cucumber, bell pepper, and greens in the center.
    - Roll tightly, seal, and slice.

Crab Stick Roll

Ingredients

- **For the Sushi Rice:**
    - 2 cups sushi rice
    - 2 ½ cups water
    - ¼ cup rice vinegar
    - 2 tablespoons sugar
    - 1 teaspoon salt
- **For the Filling:**
    - 8 ounces imitation crab sticks, shredded
    - ½ cucumber, julienned
    - ½ avocado, sliced
    - 2 tablespoons mayonnaise (optional)
- **For Rolling:**
    - 4 sheets of nori (seaweed)

Instructions

1. **Prepare the Sushi Rice:**
    - Rinse the sushi rice, cook it, and season as mentioned above. Allow to cool.
2. **Assemble the Roll:**
    - Lay a sheet of nori on a bamboo mat. Spread rice over it, leaving a 1-inch border.
    - In the center, layer shredded crab, cucumber, avocado, and drizzle with mayonnaise if using.
    - Roll tightly, seal, and slice.

Pineapple Sushi

Ingredients

- **For the Sushi Rice:**
    - 2 cups sushi rice
    - 2 ½ cups water
    - ¼ cup rice vinegar
    - 2 tablespoons sugar
    - 1 teaspoon salt
- **For the Filling:**
    - 1 cup fresh pineapple, sliced into strips
    - ½ avocado, sliced
    - 1 tablespoon shredded coconut (optional)
- **For Rolling:**
    - 4 sheets of nori (seaweed) or fruit leather for a sweeter version

Instructions

1. **Prepare the Sushi Rice:**
    - Rinse the sushi rice, cook it, and season as mentioned above. Allow to cool.
2. **Assemble the Roll:**
    - Lay a sheet of nori (or fruit leather) on a bamboo mat. Spread rice over it, leaving a 1-inch border.
    - In the center, layer pineapple strips, avocado, and sprinkle with shredded coconut if desired.
    - Roll tightly, seal, and slice.

Teriyaki Chicken Roll

Ingredients

- **For the Sushi Rice:**
    - 2 cups sushi rice
    - 2 ½ cups water
    - ¼ cup rice vinegar
    - 2 tablespoons sugar
    - 1 teaspoon salt
- **For the Filling:**
    - 1 pound boneless, skinless chicken thighs
    - ½ cup teriyaki sauce
    - ½ cucumber, julienned
    - ½ avocado, sliced
    - 4 sheets of nori (seaweed)

Instructions

1. **Prepare the Sushi Rice:**
    - Rinse the sushi rice, cook it, and season as mentioned above. Allow to cool.
2. **Cook the Chicken:**
    - Marinate chicken in teriyaki sauce for at least 30 minutes.
    - Grill or pan-fry the chicken until fully cooked, then slice into strips.
3. **Assemble the Roll:**
    - Lay a sheet of nori on a bamboo mat. Spread a layer of sushi rice, leaving a 1-inch border.
    - In the center, add teriyaki chicken, cucumber, and avocado.
    - Roll tightly, seal, and slice.

Sweet Potato Roll

Ingredients

- **For the Sushi Rice:**
    - 2 cups sushi rice
    - 2 ½ cups water
    - ¼ cup rice vinegar
    - 2 tablespoons sugar
    - 1 teaspoon salt
- **For the Filling:**
    - 1 medium sweet potato, peeled and cut into matchsticks
    - 1 tablespoon olive oil
    - Salt to taste
    - 4 sheets of nori (seaweed)

Instructions

1. **Prepare the Sushi Rice:**
    - Rinse the sushi rice, cook it, and season as mentioned above. Allow to cool.
2. **Roast the Sweet Potato:**
    - Preheat oven to 425°F (220°C). Toss sweet potato matchsticks with olive oil and salt. Spread on a baking sheet and roast for 20-25 minutes until tender.
3. **Assemble the Roll:**
    - Lay a sheet of nori on a bamboo mat. Spread rice over it, leaving a 1-inch border.
    - In the center, place roasted sweet potato.
    - Roll tightly, seal, and slice.

Sesame Spinach Roll

Ingredients

- **For the Sushi Rice:**
    - 2 cups sushi rice
    - 2 ½ cups water
    - ¼ cup rice vinegar
    - 2 tablespoons sugar
    - 1 teaspoon salt
- **For the Filling:**
    - 2 cups fresh spinach
    - 1 tablespoon sesame oil
    - 1 tablespoon sesame seeds
    - 4 sheets of nori (seaweed)

Instructions

1. **Prepare the Sushi Rice:**
    - Rinse the sushi rice, cook it, and season as mentioned above. Allow to cool.
2. **Sauté the Spinach:**
    - In a skillet, heat sesame oil over medium heat. Add spinach and cook until wilted. Sprinkle with sesame seeds.
3. **Assemble the Roll:**
    - Lay a sheet of nori on a bamboo mat. Spread rice over it, leaving a 1-inch border.
    - In the center, place the sautéed spinach.
    - Roll tightly, seal, and slice.

Poke Bowl Sushi

Ingredients

- **For the Sushi Rice:**
    - 2 cups sushi rice
    - 2 ½ cups water
    - ¼ cup rice vinegar
    - 2 tablespoons sugar
    - 1 teaspoon salt
- **For the Poke Bowl:**
    - 8 ounces sushi-grade tuna or salmon, cubed
    - 2 tablespoons soy sauce
    - 1 teaspoon sesame oil
    - 1 avocado, sliced
    - ½ cucumber, sliced
    - 1 radish, thinly sliced
    - 2 green onions, sliced
    - Seaweed salad (optional)

Instructions

1. **Prepare the Sushi Rice:**
    - Rinse the sushi rice, cook it, and season as mentioned above. Allow to cool.
2. **Marinate the Fish:**
    - In a bowl, combine cubed fish, soy sauce, and sesame oil. Let marinate for 15 minutes.
3. **Assemble the Poke Bowl:**
    - In a bowl, place a base of sushi rice. Top with marinated fish, avocado, cucumber, radish, green onions, and seaweed salad.

Kimchi Roll

Ingredients

- **For the Sushi Rice:**
    - 2 cups sushi rice
    - 2 ½ cups water
    - ¼ cup rice vinegar
    - 2 tablespoons sugar
    - 1 teaspoon salt
- **For the Filling:**
    - 1 cup kimchi, chopped
    - ½ cucumber, julienned
    - 4 sheets of nori (seaweed)

Instructions

1. **Prepare the Sushi Rice:**
    - Rinse the sushi rice, cook it, and season as mentioned above. Allow to cool.
2. **Assemble the Roll:**
    - Lay a sheet of nori on a bamboo mat. Spread rice over it, leaving a 1-inch border.
    - In the center, add chopped kimchi and cucumber.
    - Roll tightly, seal, and slice.

Quinoa Sushi

Ingredients

- **For the Quinoa:**
    - 1 cup quinoa, rinsed
    - 2 cups water
    - ¼ cup rice vinegar
    - 1 tablespoon sugar
    - 1 teaspoon salt
- **For the Filling:**
    - ½ cucumber, julienned
    - ½ avocado, sliced
    - 1 carrot, julienned
    - 4 sheets of nori (seaweed)

Instructions

1. **Prepare the Quinoa:**
    - In a pot, combine quinoa and water. Bring to a boil, then reduce heat and simmer for 15 minutes. Allow to cool.
    - Mix quinoa with vinegar, sugar, and salt.
2. **Assemble the Roll:**
    - Lay a sheet of nori on a bamboo mat. Spread a layer of quinoa over it, leaving a 1-inch border.
    - In the center, add cucumber, avocado, and carrot.
    - Roll tightly, seal, and slice.

Cilantro Lime Shrimp Roll

Ingredients

- **For the Sushi Rice:**
    - 2 cups sushi rice
    - 2 ½ cups water
    - ¼ cup rice vinegar
    - 2 tablespoons sugar
    - 1 teaspoon salt
- **For the Filling:**
    - 8 ounces shrimp, cooked and chopped
    - Juice of 1 lime
    - ¼ cup chopped cilantro
    - ½ avocado, sliced
    - 4 sheets of nori (seaweed)

Instructions

1. **Prepare the Sushi Rice:**
    - Rinse the sushi rice, cook it, and season as mentioned above. Allow to cool.
2. **Mix Shrimp Filling:**
    - In a bowl, combine chopped shrimp, lime juice, and cilantro.
3. **Assemble the Roll:**
    - Lay a sheet of nori on a bamboo mat. Spread rice over it, leaving a 1-inch border.
    - In the center, add shrimp mixture and avocado.
    - Roll tightly, seal, and slice.

Sushi Sandwich

Ingredients

- **For the Sushi Rice:**
    - 2 cups sushi rice
    - 2 ½ cups water
    - ¼ cup rice vinegar
    - 2 tablespoons sugar
    - 1 teaspoon salt
- **For the Filling:**
    - ½ cucumber, sliced
    - ½ avocado, sliced
    - ½ carrot, grated
    - 4 sheets of nori (seaweed)

Instructions

1. **Prepare the Sushi Rice:**
    - Rinse the sushi rice, cook it, and season as mentioned above. Allow to cool.
2. **Assemble the Sandwich:**
    - Lay two sheets of nori on a clean surface. Spread a thin layer of sushi rice over each.
    - In the center, layer cucumber, avocado, and carrot.
    - Place the other two nori sheets on top to create a sandwich.
    - Slice into squares or triangles.

Sweet Chili Sauce Roll

Ingredients

- **For the Sushi Rice:**
    - 2 cups sushi rice
    - 2 ½ cups water
    - ¼ cup rice vinegar
    - 2 tablespoons sugar
    - 1 teaspoon salt
- **For the Filling:**
    - 1 cup cooked shrimp or chicken, chopped
    - ¼ cup sweet chili sauce
    - ½ cucumber, julienned
    - 4 sheets of nori (seaweed)

Instructions

1. **Prepare the Sushi Rice:**
    - Rinse the sushi rice, cook it, and season as mentioned above. Allow to cool.
2. **Mix Filling:**
    - In a bowl, combine chopped shrimp or chicken with sweet chili sauce.
3. **Assemble the Roll:**
    - Lay a sheet of nori on a bamboo mat. Spread rice over it, leaving a 1-inch border.
    - In the center, add the sweet chili mixture and cucumber.
    - Roll tightly, seal, and slice.

Coconut Shrimp Roll

Ingredients

- **For the Sushi Rice:**
    - 2 cups sushi rice
    - 2 ½ cups water
    - ¼ cup rice vinegar
    - 2 tablespoons sugar
    - 1 teaspoon salt
- **For the Filling:**
    - 1 cup cooked coconut shrimp (shrimp coated with shredded coconut and fried)
    - ½ avocado, sliced
    - ½ cucumber, julienned
    - 4 sheets of nori (seaweed)

Instructions

1. **Prepare the Sushi Rice:**
    - Rinse the sushi rice, cook it, and season as mentioned above. Allow to cool.
2. **Assemble the Roll:**
    - Lay a sheet of nori on a bamboo mat. Spread rice over it, leaving a 1-inch border.
    - In the center, add coconut shrimp, avocado, and cucumber.
    - Roll tightly, seal, and slice.

www.ingramcontent.com/pod-product-compliance
Lightning Source LLC
LaVergne TN
LVHW081320060526
838201LV00055B/2381